Mushrooms & Fungi for Kids

An Introduction to Mycology

Ariel Bonkoski

Acknowledgments

I want to thank Brooks, Chester, Raechel, and Rylee for their endless support in everything that I do. I would not have been able to accomplish all that I have without your support. You all have always been there to adventure with me and learn with me, and I am forever grateful! Looking forward to future adventures with you!

Special thanks to Tavis Lynch, Justin Hammers, Alan Rockefeller, Olga Katic, and Arleen Bessette for volunteering images for this project.

Preface

I wanted to write this book because it is something I wish was available to me when I was a kid. I did not develop an interest in fungi until I was an adult. Even though I loved getting nature books when I was younger, I never even saw a book about fungi for kids! Getting young kids interested in the fascinating world of fungi will always be exciting for me.

Edited by Andrew Mollenkof

Proofread by Jenna Barron

Cover and book design by Jonathan Norberg

Photo credits page 142

10 9 8 7 6 5 4 3 2

Mushrooms & Fungi For Kids: An Introduction to Mycology

Published by Adventure Publications, an imprint of AdventureKEEN
310 Garfield Street South
Cambridge, Minnesota 55008
(800) 678-7006
www.adventurepublications.net

Printed in China
Library of Congress Control Number: 2025934232
ISBN 978-1-64755-429-3 (pbk.); 978-1-64755-430-9 (ebook)

A SAFETY NOTE

This is a guide to learning about mushrooms and fungi, not a guide to collecting mushrooms as food. Identifying edible mushrooms requires a lot of first-hand experience and knowledge, as there are many toxic or inedible mushrooms. Please do not use this book to collect mushrooms as food. Instead, join a local mushroom club, and learn directly from experts near you!

Also, before you complete any of the projects in the back of the book, keep in mind that in many places (state or local parks), disturbing any plants, wildlife, or fungi is prohibited, so be sure to know the rules where you are, respect private property, and make sure you have your parents' permission before completing any projects in this book.

Finally, stay aware of your surroundings, especially if potentially hazardous critters (snakes, for example) are found in your area, and always be on the lookout for poison ivy, ticks, and other less-than-fun finds! Always have an adult with you for supervision for safety's sake!

Table of Contents

My Mushroom Awakening

It may be surprising, but I didn't like mushrooms very much growing up. At dinner, if grocery-store mushrooms even touched my plate I treated the whole thing as contaminated!

Later, as a young adult, I worked in a restaurant that featured a lot of mushrooms in its meals. My coworkers joked with me about how I didn't like mushrooms, until one day a coworker started asking why. I told them that there was no huge explanation, they just weren't my favorite, but they explained that only a couple of different kinds of mushrooms are typically sold in grocery stores. "In nature," they continued, "there are so many wild mushrooms." He told me about a mushroom called "chicken of the woods," which made me curious, so I looked it up, and discovered it was real, and it was beautiful! It had lovely bright yellows and oranges.

At that point, I wanted to see more! So, I joined some online platforms for mushroom

Champignon mushrooms

identification just so I could see more pretty mushrooms. I was part of those groups for a while, and some mushrooms were common enough that they occasionally showed up multiple times a day. I started getting familiar with those pretty quickly!

Not long after that, while I was hiking the Superior Hiking Trail in northern Minnesota, I came across a bright orange blob in the middle of the trail. I immediately recognized it as a lobster mushroom! Because I was not an experienced mushroom hunter, I decided to buy a mushroom foraging book in town so I could send photos to experienced mushroom foragers and confirm my identification. According to the book and the experienced foragers, my identification was correct. I LOVED FINDING IT. From that moment, I found myself drawn deeper and deeper into the world of mushrooms!

For the rest of my trip along the Superior Hiking Trail, I used my new mushroom foraging book to practice identifying mushrooms we found. Later, I used the book to practice identifying mushrooms when people would post pictures online.

A lobster mushroom

Identification became a fun game to me, and I quickly became obsessed.

That's why I wrote this book—to introduce people to the world of fungi and mushrooms. Let me be clear: **This is not a guide to collecting mushrooms for food.** (Read that part again!) Instead, this book is an introduction to the weird, wild world of mushrooms and fungi. Whether we recognize it or not, we're surrounded by fungi, but too often, our idea of what a mushroom is remains misleading, simplistic, or just plain boring. The world of mushrooms and fungi is a lot more fun, colorful, and flat-out weird than we think. Come along and see what's out there to discover!

Brightly colored chicken of the woods

Introduction

This book is broken down into three main parts. The first part of this book covers general information about fungi so that you can familiarize yourself with the different kinds of fungi, what their functions are, and unique information about them. The middle section of the book highlights some mushrooms that can be found in most places in North America. This section is not a complete field guide by any means but will give you a starting point for some mushrooms. The third section of this book has different hands-on activities that you can do with mushrooms!

DISCOVERING MUSHROOMS AND FUNGI: AN INTRODUCTION TO MYCOLOGY

Mycology is the scientific study of fungi, which are a diverse group of lifeforms that includes yeasts, molds, mushrooms, and more! Some are too small to see without a microscope (microorganisms), while others are easy to spot (macroorganisms).

Lion's mane fungal colonies on a Petri dish

Fungi play important roles in various ecosystems, as they are involved in decomposition, recycling nutrients, and special relationships with plants (known as symbiosis). Mycologists, or scientists who specialize in mycology, explore the biology, taxonomy (organization), ecology (relationships with other lifeforms), and medical significance of fungi.

THE KINGDOM FUNGI

Imagine a mysterious kingdom where some of the weirdest and most amazing living things live. It's called the Kingdom Fungi, and it's a hidden world right under our feet! Fungi include mushrooms, molds, and yeasts. They can occur in every environment on Earth and play very important roles in most ecosystems. Fungi are our friends, too! Yeast helps bakers make bread fluffy, and they're behind the scenes in the making of other delicious things like pizza dough. Some of us enjoy eating grocery-store mushrooms in our soups or pastas! So, grab your magnifying glass, put on your adventure hat, and let's explore the magical Kingdom Fungi together!

Fungi are a group of eukaryotic organisms—all eukaryotes have a membrane-bound nucleus. The nucleus is the part of a cell that holds an organism's DNA, and the membrane is a barrier that lets some things in but not others. Plants and animals are also eukaryotes *(say it, yoo-carry-oats)*. What sets fungi apart from plants and animals is their special cell structure. Almost all fungi have cell walls made of chitin (the same thing that makes insect shells hard). Fungi also do not move during their life, don't contain chlorophyll, and are larger than bacteria. The rules on what's considered a fungi have actually changed over the years as scientists have learned more, so some things that used to be considered fungi no longer are. Slime molds (see page 15) are one cool example!

A close-up look at some shaggy mane mushrooms

One exciting thing about mycology is that it is a fairly new field of study, at least in North America. Fungi have been closely studied in places like Europe and Asia for many years. But when mycologists started working in North America, they assumed we had many of the same mushroom species as in Europe because they looked nearly identical. In recent years, mycologists have been studying the DNA of different fungi and have discovered that this isn't actually true! A lot of mushrooms in North America are actually different species than those found in Europe. This has resulted in lots of species name changes and other unexpected discoveries. If you keep studying and become a community/citizen scientist or a mycologist, you may just make some discoveries yourself!

WHERE DO FUNGI GROW?

Fungi can grow anywhere in the world, even Antarctica! They can grow in dry conditions like in deserts or, rarely, even underwater. As mentioned earlier, you can also find fungi growing on spoiled food or in water-damaged buildings. Most of the time, though, you find fungi out in nature. To find mushrooms near you, look around your yard or visit a local park with an adult.

Some mushrooms even grow on lawns.

TYPES OF FUNGI

There are a few different types of fungi. There are molds, yeasts, smuts (yes, that's a real word!), and mushrooms. There are also slime molds, which used to be considered fungi until they were moved to a different kingdom. Let's cover their basic differences.

Mushrooms A mushroom is the reproductive fruiting body of a much larger organism. Mushrooms grow from mycelium, which are fungal strands typically found in soil or wood. Mycelium is very thin and splits in all different directions and can look similar to a spider's web! Because of that, we usually don't see it, as it is often found within or beneath soil or wood. We just see the mushroom when it appears aboveground! You don't have to study fungi for long to see that mushrooms can take on many different shapes, colors, sizes, and textures.

FUNGI THAT DON'T PRODUCE MUSHROOMS

Not every fungi produces a mushroom. Examples of fungi that don't include molds, yeasts, and even fungi that can grow on people. Yes, fungi can live in between your toes. (We usually call it "athlete's foot.")

Molds We have all probably seen food that's been on the kitchen counter or in the fridge for too long, and it starts to develop strangely colored spots or even becomes kind of hairy or powdery. That's mold! We usually think "yuck" and throw it away as quickly as possible without giving it much thought. But while you're on the way to toss those moldy strawberries into the trash, keep in mind: that mold is a fungus! There are many types of molds out there, but most people are only familiar with food molds. Molds can occur on our foods, in our bathrooms, or in nature. They can show up just about anywhere!

Yeasts Yeasts are made of egg-shaped fungi cells that are so small you can't see them without a microscope! They usually are found in soils or on plants. They especially like sugar, so yeast is often found on fruits or sweet flower nectar. People use yeast when making bread, beer and wine, root beer, and many other products.

Lichen Lichen are part fungi, part plant—they are basically a team that consists of algae and several types of fungi. Lichen can occur in many different shapes, sizes, colors, and patterns. Some even can grow on bare rock! Some lichen species can look like mushrooms, but others look more like plants.

Slime Molds Slime molds aren't actually fungi, but they were once considered to be fungi. Scientifically, slime molds now belong to a different kingdom, Protista (the Protists). You might be thinking, "Why are molds a fungus, but slime molds are not?" The answer has to do with their cells: Slime molds have cell structures that differ from true molds or fungi.

There are other differences too: Slime molds don't penetrate the substrate (the surface they live on) with hyphae (branching filaments) like mushrooms do (see page 16). Instead, they form plasmodia, which can move across organic matter or non-organic matter. (You read that right, slime molds can move!) But they do have a spore stage similar to that of mushrooms. Because they are so neat, we will cover a few common slime molds in the field guide portion of the book!

Fungal mycelial colonies often look like thin "roots."

HOW MUSHROOMS REPRODUCE

An individual mushroom is basically a fruit (or fruit-body). Fruit doesn't just appear—it is part of a larger organism. When it comes to fungi, that larger organism is called the mycelial *(say it, my-cell-ee-ul)* colony, a network of very thin filaments called hyphae. These root-like structures connect and then branch in different directions and spread nutrients and oxygen throughout the mycelium. We usually don't see the mycelial colony because it is in whatever substrate the mushroom is growing on. The mushrooms are the fruiting body of the fungus. Imagine an apple growing from an apple tree: it is quite similar to that. The apple is like a mushroom, and the apple tree is like an entire fungus.

Mushrooms can reproduce sexually or asexually. Asexual reproduction can be a fairly simple process. In some cases, the mycelium (think "fungal roots") breaks apart into different segments and can grow from there.

Sexual reproduction is a bit more complicated and rather unique. Some fungi produce mushrooms to help themselves reproduce. Mushrooms contain something similar to seeds—they are called spores. Spores are tiny, and you need a microscope to see an individual spore. Most mushrooms release a huge number of spores, which are blown around by the wind. Mushrooms need to produce a lot of spores, as most don't land in a spot where they can reproduce. Some mushrooms can release more than a million spores a day! When a spore lands somewhere it can grow, it will begin to germinate, or grow. Hyphae will grow out from the spore and form a brand-new mycelial colony. Then, when two mycelial colonies combine themselves, they are ready to form mushrooms and keep the cycle going!

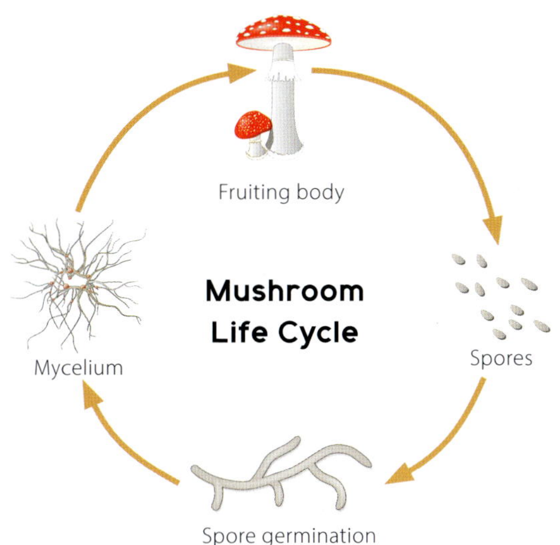

BASIDIOMYCETES VS. ASCOMYCETES

There are two main groups of fungi, and those groups are based on their spore shape. **Basidiomycetes** *(say it, buh-city-oh-my-seats)* have spores that form on a structure called a basidia. Basidia are often kind of club-shaped, but there is some variety in their shape. The basidia often have one to eight spores each. **Ascomycetes** *(say it, asco-my-seats)* form spores within microscopic cells called asci. Each ascus is round or cubed in shape and can hold a varying number of spores, from one to over a hundred! Because of this, some fungi species can produce many more spores than other species. With a microscope, it's possible to see these spores, and mycologists often use microscopes to help identify fungi!

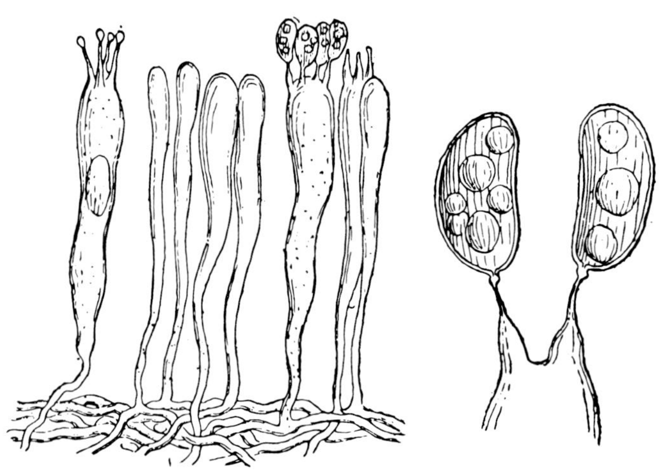

Left: Basidiomycetes have basidia (club-shaped structures) that hold spores.
Right: Ascomycetes have asci, round or cup-shaped cells that hold spores.

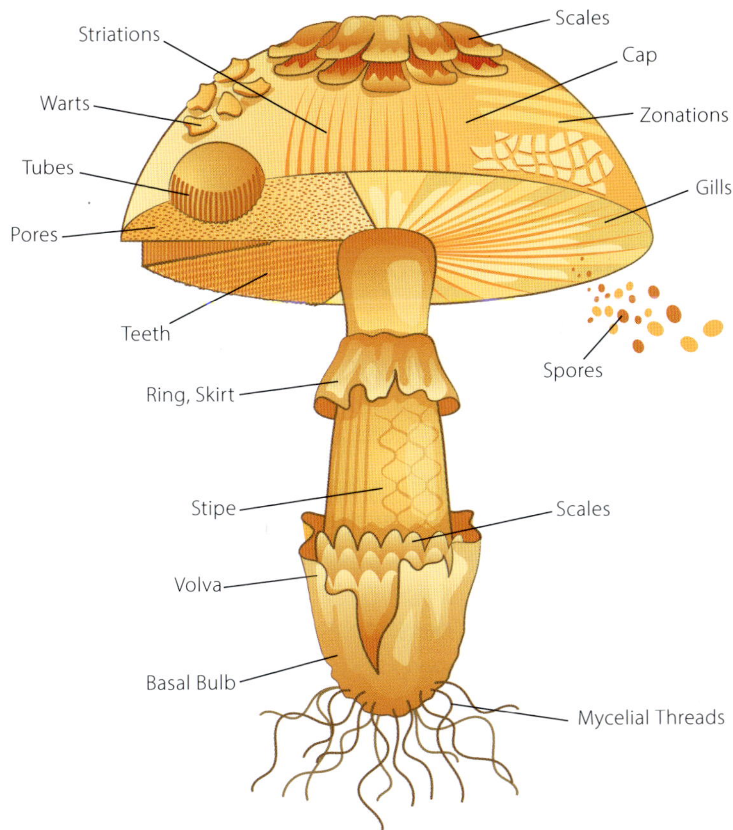

MUSHROOM ANATOMY

Mushrooms can have many different features, and not all mushrooms have the same ones. But if you want to learn about mushrooms, it's helpful to know about the structures that many mushrooms share.

Note: Not every mushroom has all of the features shown in the mushroom above, but they are important terms to know!

Cap Many mushrooms have a cap. The cap is the tissue that covers the top of the mushroom. Caps can have many different patterns or textures, such as concentric (circular) zones or rings, warts, scales, or striations (grooves or scratches). Caps can be fleshy or even woody.

Underside (spore-bearing surface) Mushrooms with caps have an underside to the cap. This is where it releases the spores that help it reproduce. The underside may have gills, pores, or tooth-like shapes. These patterns are often important to identifying the mushroom.

Stipe The stipe is the mushroom's stem. It can have unique features or textures. The stipe could be scaly, fuzzy, spotted, shaggy, reticulated (with a net-like pattern), and so on. It can be very prominent or sometimes hard to see at first glance.

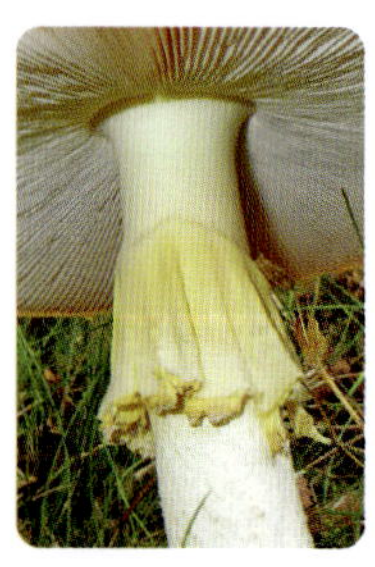

Skirts and Veils One unique feature you may see on the stipe of some mushrooms is a skirt or ring. Skirts or rings can be fleshy and hang from the mushroom, almost like a real skirt, while others can be cobweb-like. If you see a skirt, that means that the bottom of that skirt was once connected to the edge of the cap, and it broke away as the mushroom matured. When that skirt is still connected to the edge of the cap, that's called a veil. It is called a veil because it covers up the true underside of the mushroom.

Basal Bulb or Universal Veil Some mushrooms start growing in a ball or egg shape and eventually, the rest of the mushroom will emerge from that "egg". That "egg" is known as a basal bulb or universal veil. This unique feature is located at the base of the mushroom. When that basal bulb is left at the base of the mushroom as it matures, that is called a volva.

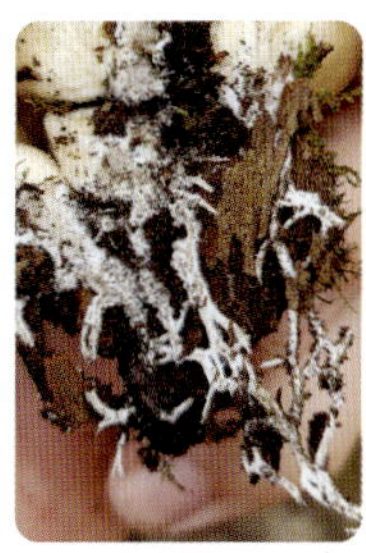

Mycelial Cords or Rhizomorphs Mushrooms don't have roots, but if you see what looks like roots at the base of a mushroom, those are mycelial cords. Mycelial cords connect the mycelium to the mushroom fruiting body.

TYPES OF MUSHROOMS

Mushrooms are often grouped together by their appearance, and if you want to learn about fungi, it's helpful to learn about these general categories. But keep in mind that just because a mushroom is lumped into a group, it doesn't mean it's closely related or has the same family. (Plus, there are some strange/odd mushrooms that don't fall into any real category, but because they are more unique, they can be easier to identify.)

Gilled Mushrooms Gilled mushrooms are what most people think of when they think of a mushroom. Gilled mushrooms are fleshy and typically have a stipe (a stem), a cap, and gills that are located underneath the cap. Gills are blade-like structures that extend from the center of the cap toward the edge or the other way around.

Polypore or Shelf Mushrooms Polypores *(say it, paul-e-poors)* are leathery, woody, or tough mushrooms that grow from wood and typically have pores on the underside of their cap. Other polypores have a gilled structure beneath their cap, and some have a stipe. In most polypores, the pores are difficult to separate from the cap. Polypores are sometimes called shelf mushrooms because they often look like a shelf coming out of the wood.

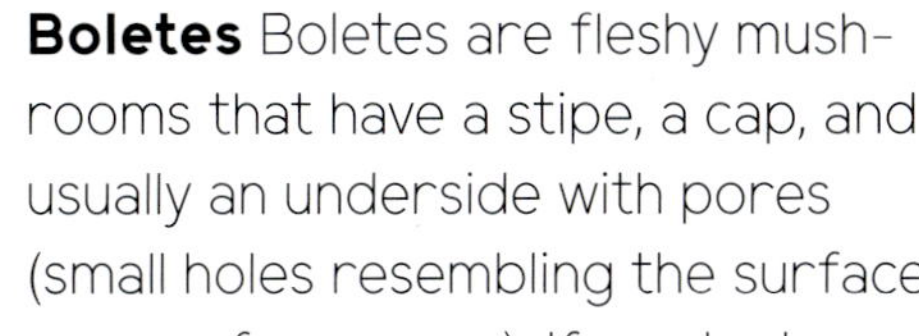

Boletes Boletes are fleshy mushrooms that have a stipe, a cap, and usually an underside with pores (small holes resembling the surface of a sponge). If you look closely, the pores are composed of tightly compacted individual tubes.

Toothed Mushrooms Toothed mushrooms are fleshy or woody and have teeth, or spines, on them. Sometimes, these teeth can be located on the underside of a cap, or the mushroom can be irregularly shaped with teeth all over.

Coral Mushrooms Coral mushrooms are fleshy or fragile mushrooms with branches that resemble sea coral.

Crust Mushrooms Crust mushrooms usually grow on wood, and they are often flat. As you might have guessed from the name, it looks like a crust on the surface where it's found. The exposed crust can be smooth, wrinkled, bumpy, or have pores.

Jelly Mushrooms Jelly mushrooms are moist jelly-like mushrooms. They take on many forms, most commonly growing like a blob, but they sometimes can take on almost a coral-like or lobed shape. When these are fresh, the texture reminds me of wet gummy bears!

Puffball Mushrooms Puffball mushrooms are ball-shaped when mature. Their size can vary depending on the species, ranging from as small as a pea to larger than a basketball.

Cup Mushrooms Cup mushrooms are fleshy mushrooms with a cup shape.

Stinkhorn Mushrooms Stinkhorn mushrooms are mushrooms that smell bad. Not all mushrooms that smell bad are considered stinkhorns. Stinkhorns have a gross-smelling slime at some point in their life, and when they are very young, they grow from an "egg" that the rest of the mushroom emerges from as it matures. When it is in its egg stage, it can often be confused with a puffball.

Morels and Others These are mushrooms that have a stipe and a wrinkled or pitted cap.

FUNGI IN THE ECOSYSTEM

Fungi play many crucial roles in the Earth's ecosystem. Many fungi are decomposers; they are part of nature's recycling crew. If we didn't have them helping to break down dead wood and leaf litter, there would likely be more frequent or severe wildfires. Since they help break things down, they also help create healthy soils. Farmers also sometimes use fungi-rich soil to grow nutritious food! One of the most obvious uses for fungi is as food itself. Mammals, insects, and even people eat mushrooms. Fungi can play a number of different roles in the environment.

Saprobes are the recycling crew of the woods! Saprotrophic fungi get the nutrients they need by breaking down plant matter. The fungus puts out enzymes that convert the material into simpler molecules. The fungi's cells absorb those molecules to feed themselves.

Saprobes help decompose and recycle plant materials in the forest.

Mycorrhizal fungi connect directly to tree roots, enabling the exchange of nutrients.

Mycorrhizal fungi are the "internet" of the forest! Mycorrhizal fungi get their nutrients by having a symbiotic (mutually beneficial) relationship with plants, meaning both the fungi and the plants benefit from this partnership! Mycorrhizal fungi attach their mycelium to the roots of the plants and help them both absorb nutrients. Many plants rely on these fungi to get mineral nutrients like phosphorus, sugars, or other nutrients. In forests where there are a lot of mycorrhizal fungi, the mycelium creates a network that connects many trees together and transfers nutrients as needed among the trees.

Parasitic fungi are the vampires of the woods. Parasitic fungi get their nutrients by attacking living hosts like plants or animals (often insects). Sometimes, they even attack other fungi! Parasitic fungi enter their host through some sort of opening or wound. The fungus then feeds on the organism's cytoplasm, which leads to disease or the organism's death!

FUNGI, INSECTS, AND INVERTEBRATES

Many insects and other invertebrates have unique relationships with fungi. One of the most common examples is that many insects and other invertebrates, like snails and slugs, may eat mushrooms or even just the spores of the mushrooms. That is why you can often find mushrooms that have nibbles taken out of them, and it's also why you'll often see insects on mushrooms or visible insect tunnels in mushrooms.

Many invertebrates feed directly on fungi, or even live on/in them!

Sometimes fungi can even be parasitic on various insects! Some fungi that parasitize insects completely change the behavior of the insect.

Some fungi parasitize insects and even grow out of them!

When these fungi infect an insect, it will make the insect climb to a high point before the fungi eventually kills it. Then, a mushroom fruiting body emerges from the insect. This benefits the fungi because its spores will be released from a greater height and will have a better chance of spreading and infecting other insects.

Some wasp species use fungi to help their young survive!

Some insects use fungi in more complicated ways. For example, some wasps lay their eggs deep in wood, and they'll carry fungi spores and cover the eggs in spores. As those wasp eggs mature, the fungi starts to grow in the wood and begins to decompose the wood, making it softer. When the larvae hatch, the wood will then be soft enough for them to eat!

FUNGI AND PEOPLE

Humans interact with fungi in their daily lives in many different ways. Examples include buying mushrooms at the grocery store, baking bread or pizza dough, or using some mushrooms to dye fabric or yarn. Some fungi are even used in life-saving medicines like antibiotics or anti-cancer drugs!

While fungi are often helpful, sometimes we interact with fungi in less positive ways. For example, when food stays in the fridge or on the counter for too long, it'll develop mold (a type of fungus). Mold can also grow on walls, ceilings, or on floors if there's too much moisture. Molds found in homes usually require a professional cleaning team to get rid of them fully. There are even fungi that can live on (or in) people. An example is toenail fungus, which can cause discolored, thick, or brittle toenails, which may become uncomfortable or painful. Seeing a doctor is suggested if this ever happens to you! But don't worry; while there are a few trouble-makers out there, most fungi are entirely harmless.

Some fungi, such as black mold, can be dangerous when it grows in buildings.

A NOTE TO PARENTS ABOUT SAFETY AND TOXICITY

This book is not a guide to collecting mushrooms for use as food. The reason is simple: Some fungi are edible, some are inedible, and others are toxic and

Remember, this is not a guide to collecting edible mushrooms; buy your fungi at the grocery store!

even deadly. Knowing how to safely identify mushrooms takes experience, practice, and a lot more information than we can fit into this book. If you're interested in learning more about mushrooms as food (and how to identify toxic lookalikes), join a local mushrooming club and learn first-hand from a certified expert. **Again, please do not use this book as a guide to collecting mushrooms as food.** This book has a different purpose—to introduce you to the wonderful world of fungi and mushrooms.

And good news: Regardless of their edibility or toxicity, all mushrooms are safe to touch, unless you happen to be allergic (though this is *quite* rare).

Identifying Mushrooms

When you are trying to identify a mushroom, it's important to look at all of its features. This may require picking the mushroom to see all of it properly. This is safe to do for the organism since mushrooms are just the fruiting body of the organism. It's similar to picking an apple, which doesn't harm the apple tree. Just make sure you are not damaging the environment around the mushroom or the substrate where it is growing. Many mushrooms can look alike, so for accurate identification, these are the things you should pay attention to:

Habitat What is the mushroom growing from? Is it growing from sand, soil, wood chips, a twig, a tree trunk, an underground root, or a stump? If it's growing from or near a tree, what kind of tree is it? Many mushrooms that grow from trees only grow from certain trees, so when you're trying to identify mushrooms, knowing your trees can be very helpful!

The cap (or top of the mushroom) What colors are you seeing? Are there any unique textures or patterns?

The underside Are you seeing gills, pores, or teeth? Do they have a pattern? Are they firm or flimsy? What color are they? Does the mushroom bruise when damaged or when you press on it?

The stipe (stem) What color is it? Do you see any unique textures or patterns here? Does it have a skirt? Are there any unique features at the base of the stipe? Does it bruise when damaged?

For mushrooms that don't have caps, undersides, or stipes—like some coral mushrooms, cup mushrooms, or round mushrooms—closely observe the entire mushroom from all angles and make a note of all colors, textures, and patterns that you can see.

MAKING A SPORE PRINT

Making a spore print is a great way to learn more about a mushroom. Individual spores are not large enough to see without a microscope, but when there are a lot of them, you'll be able to see their color. Spore color is important because it varies by species, and a spore print color can be used to confirm or reject an identification. So, if you have found a mushroom that you think you have identified properly and that mushroom is supposed to have white spores, and a spore print shows a different spore color than it's supposed to, you have incorrectly identified that mushroom. Please note that many mushrooms have look-alikes that have the same color spores, so this is not a definitive way to identify mushrooms; it's just one of many tools that can help with identification.

HOW TO MAKE A SPORE PRINT

You will need:

- Mushrooms with gills or pores are best. Others (coral, cup) are not likely to produce a spore print.
- Tinfoil or aluminum foil
- A cup or bowl

If your mushroom has a stipe, remove that

Then place the mushroom gills or pores face down on your foil.

Place the cup or bowl over the mushroom to block off any airflow.

You should get a spore print within 4–9 hours. It's often recommended to do the process before bed and check on your spore print when you wake up. Spore prints are not only a helpful feature to look at during the identification process, but they really can be quite beautiful, and you can even make art with them! When you're making a spore print, be careful not to bump or disturb it, as may smudge, which is just fine for observing the color of the spores, but most people don't find smudged spore prints as pretty.

Using the Field Guide Section

This field guide section introduces common and notable mushrooms that occur throughout North America. This informal field guide is organized as follows:

Mushrooms with a cap, stipe, and bold gills on the underside of the cap (page 38)

Mushrooms with a cap, stipe, and bold pores on the underside of the cap (page 52)

Mushrooms with a cap, stipe, and bold teeth on the underside of the cap (page 58)

Mushrooms with a shelf-like shape and bold pores underneath the cap (page 66)

Mushrooms with a shelf-like shape and gills on the underside of the cap (page 76)

Mushrooms with a round or ball-like shape (page 82)

Mushrooms with a club-like or coral shape (page 88)

Mushrooms that look like jelly and other unusual-looking mushrooms (page 96)

Weird, "slimy-looking" things that sort of resemble mushrooms (page 110)

Each field guide entry includes some fun information about each mushroom, as well as some tips on how to identify them. On your adventures, you will likely find many fungi not found here, but the guide will introduce to you some of the fun fungi found throughout most of North America. Finally, remember, this is **not** a guide made to help you identify mushrooms to eat, so do not eat any fungi or mushrooms you find! Instead, take pictures, make spore prints, and enjoy how weird and wild mushrooms and fungi are!

Cap/Stipe with Gills

Mushrooms that have a cap, stipe, and gills are usually what most people think of when they hear the term "mushroom" or even "toadstool." These mushrooms release spores from the gills on the underside of the mushroom to help it reproduce.

Mushrooms in this group are often fleshy and somewhat fragile. You can find them growing from wood or the ground, depending on the identification of each mushroom. This group is also probably what you will find the most of!

Golden chanterelle

Shaggy mane

BRITTLEGILLS

Brittlegills are some of the most commonly found mushrooms in North America. The name "brittlegills" doesn't apply to just one species; instead, all brittlegills belong to the *Russula* genus. Because this is a very large genus of mushrooms, they can be many different colors depending on the exact species. Sometimes, you can gather enough different brittlegills from one walk in the woods to make a rainbow with all the different colors!

Habitat: You can find brittlegills growing from soil, moss, wood, and near or on hardwoods or conifers! They usually grow individually but sometimes in groups.

Cap: The cap can come in a wide range of colors, including red, yellow, tan, orange, green, purple, gray, and more. The cap is smooth or even sticky, depending on the species. A unique feature with some brittlegills is that the cap "skin" or cuticle will peel off, though not all brittle gills will do this. The cap shape will be rounded when young but will flatten out as it ages.

Gills: The gills of brittlegills are white to a little yellowish. The gills touch the stipe.

Stipe: The stipe will be whitish, but you may see some pinkish or yellow on the stipe of some species.

Spore color: The spore color can range from white to yellowish.

Common yellow russula

Russula virescens

SHAGGY MANES

Shaggy manes are some of my favorites to find! They have a unique shape, but also do something wonderful: they deliquesce *(say it, dell-ih-kwess)* which means that when this mushroom ages, it turns into a goopy, black ooze. There are other mushrooms that do this, and they are often called "inky caps" because of it. Not surprisingly, the liquid can also make a good ink.

Habitat: Shaggy manes typically grow in grassy soil or sometimes in wood chips, growing alone or in clusters.

Cap: The cap is white and cylindrical around the stipe and has shaggy white scales, which is where it gets its common name from! As it ages, the cap will widen a bit as it starts the deliquescence process until the cap completely liquifies.

Gills: The gills start out whitish, then start to turn pink as they age. As the mushroom starts the deliquescence stage, they turn black. The gills also do not actually touch the stipe; they end just before reaching the stipe.

Stipe: The white stipe ranges in height (some are tall, some short) and has a delicate white ring that is often near the base.

Spore color: The spore color is black. Please note that because this mushroom turns into goo, collecting spores is very difficult, and you will usually only get a pile of black liquid.

A shaggy mane deliquescing (turning to inky goo)

GOLDEN CHANTERELLES

For many people, golden chanterelles are what inspired their interest in wild mushrooms!

Habitat: Chanterelles grow from soil near hardwoods or conifers.

Cap: The golden/yellowish cap is rounded when young, and starts to flatten out, eventually becoming more flute-shaped and having a depressed center when it's most mature. The cap is smooth.

Gills: The gills of golden chanterelles are unique. They are called "false gills." While they are technically still gills, they are more vein-like or blunted than typical gills (which are blade like). The gills can be the same golden/yellow as the cap, and sometimes these gills are much paler, almost white. The gills can also fork, splitting off into different directions.

Chanterelle gills

Stipe: The stipe is sometimes the same color as the gills, but it can be even paler to white. The stipe is smooth.

Spore color: The spores are whitish to pale yellow.

Chanterelles viewed from above (left) and (right) with the "false" gills showing

LILAC OYSTERLING

Lilac oysterlings are a fun find due to their purple color! Even though it has a cap, stipe, and gills, scientists have recently learned that it's more closely related to shelf mushrooms with pores (page 66).

Habitat: You can find lilac oysterlings on dead hardwood, growing alone or in clusters.

Cap: The cap is smooth and flat when young but will become funnel shaped as it ages and grows up to a couple of inches across. Sometimes, it also has a yellowish or tan spot in the center as it ages.

Gills: The gills are purple when young but fade to yellow, tan, or white as they age, but the individual gills may still have some purple on the edge or margin. The gills run down the stipe a little bit.

Stipe: The short stipe is usually centered or slightly off-center. It is purple and may be fuzzy.

Spore color: The spore color is white.

Lilac oysterlings growing amid a decaying log

Lilac oysterlings of different ages: mature (on the left), and younger individuals (right).

PARROT WAXCAP

This mushroom is known for being very slimy! It's so slimy that it's often hard to pick because it can just slip out of your fingers! This mushroom gets its common name because it's the same color as some parrots.

Habitat: It grows from soil, alone or sometimes scattered near others.

Cap: The cap is almost cone-shaped or rounded when young but flattens a bit as it ages, still keeping the bump in the middle. It is green, yellow, reddish, orange, or pink. The cap is slimy.

Gills: The gills are yellow with some white or other colors. The gills are spaced out with small, notched gills from the edge.

Stipe: The short, thin stipe is usually yellow with a hint of green or other colors. The stipe is smooth and slimy.

Spore color: The spore color is white.

Parrot waxcaps can have a parrot-like green color.

Parrot waxcaps are often slimy.

BLEWIT

The blewit is another fun purple mushroom. Some people say it smells like orange juice or even lilac flowers. This is a mushroom that has many purple lookalikes, so pay close attention to the identification features when identifying this one!

Habitat: Blewits grow alone or near others in organic debris, like leaves or conifer needles.

Cap: The smooth cap is rounded or flat with a bump in the middle. It is a soft purple but develops some gray or tan spots as it ages.

Gills: The gills start out purple but fade to a light brownish color as the mushroom ages.

Stipe: The smooth stipe is short with a bulbous base and is a pale purple.

Spore color: The spore color is white.

Blewits are sometimes found in clusters. The gills are gorgeous, too!

Cap/Stipe with Pores

Mushrooms that have a cap, stipe, and pores on the underside are often called boletes *(say it, bo-leets)*. Boletes are typically fleshy and can be somewhat fragile. Most boletes grow from soil, but there are some that can grow from wood. Boletes release spores from their pores. If you look very closely, you will see that the pores are made up of tightly packed individual tubes!

Bolete pores

Birch bolete

PEPPERY BOLETE

This bolete gets its name from its peppery flavor (but please don't taste it)!

Habitat: The peppery bolete grows alone or near others in the soil near pine trees.

Cap: The cap is a bit cone-shaped when young but is otherwise more rounded on top, sometimes flattening with age. It is a reddish-brown, orangish, or a pale tan. It can sometimes feel like suede (soft leather) when young but will become smooth or even cracked with age.

Pores: The pores are yellow but sometimes have hints of orange, red, or pink and when bruised, show a darker brown.

Stipe: The thin stipe has streaks of color that can range from reddish brown to orangish or yellow.

Spore color: The spore color ranges from rusty brown to olive brown.

When identifying these mushrooms, observe from every angle you can!

BIRCH BOLETE

This mushroom is named for growing near birch trees! This is another mushroom that has many lookalikes. Many of the lookalikes may simply have a different color cap, such as reds, oranges, whitish, etc. So observe closely!

Habitat: Birch bolete can grow alone or near others. It grows from soil near birch trees.

Cap: The cap is rounded but may flatten out with age. It can be different shades of brown or gray. It will feel like suede (soft leather) or even grainy. May bruise reddish, gray, or blue when cut open.

Pores: The pores are whitish to brownish and may bruise brown. The pores are roundish.

Stipe: The stipe starts very short but can reach to several inches tall. It will usually be slightly wider at the base than at the top, where it connects to the pores. It will be whitish with black-dotted scales (also known as scabers). It can bruise blue, gray, or reddish when cut open or damaged.

Spore color: The spore color is brown.

Two views of birch boletes and their characteristic scales and pore surfaces

Cap/Stipe with Teeth/Spines

Mushrooms that have a cap, stem, and teeth on the underside are often called "toothed" mushrooms. These teeth can range in shape from very skinny and round to thicker and wide. The teeth or spines release spores to help the mushroom reproduce. These mushrooms can grow from wood or soil.

Wood hedgehog

Bleeding tooth

HEDGEHOGS

This mushroom is named for its toothy underside, which resembles a hedgehog!

Habitat: These grow alone or in clusters from soil near hardwoods or conifers.

Cap: The cap is typically rounded but can have a depressed center and occasional bumps. The cap color can range from creamy white to tan to orangish.

Teeth: The teeth start out quite short and become longer and shaggier as the mushroom ages. They can range from white, yellow to tan, to almost orangish.

The teeth end where they meet the stipe and do not run down the stipe.

Stipe: The smooth stipe is centered or just off center and creamy to tan or yellowish tan in color. The stem's thickness is uneven and wider in some spots. It is usually wider at the base.

Spore color: The spore color is white.

From the top or the side, hedeghog mushrooms might look like a "normal" mushroom, but look for their teeth underneath the cap!

HAWK WINGS

Hawk wings are super-fun mushrooms to find, thanks to their unique scaly caps and toothy undersides.

Habitat: Hawk wings can grow alone or in clusters. They grow near conifers or rarely hardwoods.

Cap: The cap can be variable in size, growing as large as 10 inches across. It is rounded with a depressed center. The cap has very prominent raised scales that can be dark brown or even blackish. Under the scales, the cap is a pale to brownish color.

Teeth: The teeth run down the stipe a bit. They start out very short and pale brown when young but become a darker brown and longer as they age.

Stipe: The stipe can be a few centimeters tall to a few inches tall. It can be smooth to faintly textured and pale to darker brown in color.

Spore color: The spore color is brown.

Hawk wings have scaly caps and are densely toothed underneath.

BLEEDING TOOTH

This is one of the most eye-catching mushrooms out there when it is young because it bleeds! Now, mushrooms don't actually have blood; what's happening is called guttation *(say it, gut-ation)*, which is when an organism has too much moisture and excretes liquid, creating beads of moisture on its exterior.

Habitat: Bleeding tooth mushrooms grow on the ground near conifer trees, alone or scattered.

Cap: The white or pinkish cap starts kind of rounded but can flatten or even slightly depress in the center as it ages. It can have very dramatic lumps or divots. The cap can be very fuzzy when young but can become velvety as it ages. Sometimes, it exudes a reddish liquid. It can be up to 4 inches across.

Teeth: The teeth start out a pale pink color but become dark brown with age. They will run down the stipe a bit. They start out very short but become longer as they age.

Stipe: The stipe is thin and reddish brown when young but can turn black with age. The texture is rough or even fuzzy, and the stipe is irregularly shaped.

Spore color: The spore color is brown.

Bleeding tooth mushrooms can be easy to spot thanks to the blood-red liquid that young specimens produce.

Shelf with Pores

Shelf-like mushrooms have pores on the underside, and they are often called "polypores." Polypores grow from wood. Sometimes they grow from the roots of trees or even buried wood, making it look like they are growing from the ground. They release their spores from their pores. A polypore's surface can range from soft and fleshy to leathery to almost as hard as a rock!

Turkey tail

Chicken of the woods

CHICKEN OF THE WOODS

Chicken of the woods is one of the most eye-catching mushrooms around due to its size and its vibrant orange-and-yellow color.

Habitat: It can grow from hardwoods or conifers. It grows in a rosette (a clustered shelf pattern).

Cap: The cap color can range from pale orange or coral to yellowish to vibrant orange and reddish orange. Sometimes it has a yellowish cap margin, and you may see subtle banding patterns of slightly different colors. The cap is smooth, sometimes soft. The cap may also be semicircular, fan-shaped, kidney-shaped, or irregularly shaped. It ranges in size, but each cap can grow up to a couple feet across. The fruiting body will usually have several caps clustered together or growing near others.

Pores: The pores are bright-to-dull yellow. The color will fade to white as it ages. One species found in the eastern US always has white pores.

Stipe: No stipe.

Spore color: The spore color is white.

Chicken of the woods is often easy to spot due to its bright cap colors. The pores can be colorful (or white) too!

ARTIST'S CONK

Artist's conk gets its name because it can be used to make art! Artists use tools to scratch into the underside of its cap, creating an etching. This etching can be preserved and displayed as art! If you want to try it yourself, see page 131 for directions!

Habitat: Artist's conk grows alone or in clustered shelves on dead hardwoods and, rarely, conifers.

Cap: The cap can get as large as a couple of feet across and will be fan-shaped or semicircular. It is very hard and will be brown to brownish gray with a white margin. The artist's conk cap also has bumps that form a banded pattern as well.

Pores: The pores are very small and white but turn dark brown when bruised or scratched.

Stipe: No stipe.

Spore color: The spore color is reddish brown or rusty brown.

Artist's conk's caps can be large. The pores are white and turn brown when scratched or etched.

DYER'S POLYPORE

This mushroom gets its common name because it is a highly prized mushroom and used to dye fabrics!

Habitat: Dyer's polypore grows from conifer trees, sometimes growing from buried roots so that it looks like it's growing from soil.

Cap: The cap starts quite small but can sometimes be larger than a foot across! It will be fan-shaped or round, and sometimes the same specimen can produce multiple caps, branching and overlapping each other. They start out bright yellow or orange yellow and develop concentric (circular) bands of color with

yellows, oranges, browns, and tans. They eventually turn completely dark brown as they age. When young, they are hairy or woolly but become smoother with age.

Pores: The small pores are bright yellow when young, sometimes more of a yellow green, and they bruise brown when damaged. The pores can have a variety of shapes, ranging from elongated to even maze-like, and the pores run down the stipe a little bit.

Stipe: The stipe is not always super visible but is brownish. Sometimes multiple stipes can fuse together. It will either be central or off-centered.

Spore color: The spore color is white or cream.

As these individuals show, dyer's polypore can vary a lot in color!

TURKEY TAIL

This mushroom gets its common name from its resemblance to a turkey's tail feathers! It has a lookalike called the false turkey tail! False turkey tail have similar banding patterns on the cap, but the underside is tan and completely smooth with no pores.

Habitat: It grows on decaying hardwood, usually in clusters, or near each other.

Cap: The cap of this mushroom will have many colors that form a banding pattern. Its pattern colors include white, brown, blue, green, red, and orange. It grows in a fan shape, or semicircle or kidney shape. It can grow in clustered rosettes or more shelf-like. The texture is hairy or velvety and may have zones of different textures. The cap is also very thin.

Pores: The pores are small and white but can turn brownish as they age.

Stipe: No stipe.

Spore color: The spore color is white.

Look for turkey tail's feather-like banding pattern and for small white pores on the underside.

Shelf with Gills

Shelf-like mushrooms that have gills on the underside often come as a surprise. From the top, most people would expect this mushroom to have pores on the underside, like most polypores. But some polypores have gills! These unique mushrooms release their spores from the gills to reproduce. Gilled polypores usually range from leathery to quite firm.

Conifer mazegill

Gilled polypore

CONIFER MAZEGILL

Conifer mazegill grows on conifers and often has maze-like gills!

Habitat: It grows from dead conifer wood, alone or near others, sometimes fusing together.

Cap: The tough cap is semicircular or fan-shaped and can be up to 4 inches across and up to 2 inches deep. It has concentric (circular) bands of different colors and textures but starts out mostly yellow, orange, and a little brown. It becomes a darker brown or almost black as it ages, and it will usually have a yellow margin until really old. The cap is velvety or hairy.

Gills: The gills start out yellow then become lighter yellow or whitish near the edge of the underside when young, while the rest is brown. It will become completely brown as it ages. The gills can split, become loose, or will have random gaps, creating a mazegill pattern.

Stipe: No stipe.

Spore color: The spore color is white.

Conifer mazegill has a yellow or brown cap and maze-like gill patterns.

GILLED POLYPORE

Gilled polypores are a very common find throughout North America.

Habitat: Gilled polypores are found on dead hardwoods and, rarely, conifers, growing alone or in clustered shelves, sometimes fusing together.

Cap: The cap is semicircular and flat to a little rounded on top. It has concentric (circular) zones of different colors or textures. It is velvety or hairy. Some colors you may see are orange, reddish orange, brown, tan, gray, whitish, or sometimes greenish if algae has grown on it. The cap is flexible when young.

Gills: The gills are whitish or creamy colored. The gills sometimes break, and you may see short gills that do not run all the way from the margin to the base of the mushroom.

Stipe: No stipe.

Spore color: The spore color is white to yellowish.

Gilled polypore has circular zones of color on the top of its cap and gills on the underside.

Round Mushrooms

Round mushrooms are very unique. Some people call all mature round mushrooms "puffballs," but not all round mushrooms fit into that grouping and there are several accepted definitions for puffballs.

Round mushrooms are a ball shape when mature, but not all round mushrooms are perfectly ball shaped. Some have a stumpy base where it connects to the soil. Ball-shaped mushrooms hold their spores inside, and as the mushroom ages, the spores develop inside and a hole forms at the top of the mushroom to let the spores out. Round mushrooms can range from squishy to firm.

Common earthball

Pear-shaped puffball

STUMP PUFFBALLS

Stump puffballs grow from tree stumps or other dead wood.

Habitat: These mushrooms are found on decaying wood and can grow alone but usually in groups. There can sometimes be hundreds in one area.

Fruiting body: Stump puffballs can be almost perfectly round, or they can have a bit of a base that may look similar to a chunky stipe. They can grow up to a couple of inches across and are white to brownish as they age. Inside, the mushroom will be white when young, later becoming yellow, then olive, and eventually develops an olive-brown powder inside, which are the spores. When young, the mushroom will be a little squishy, similar to a marsh-mallow, but will become hollower as the mushroom develops the spores inside. The outer part of the mushroom might be smooth or granular. Eventually, a hole will develop at the top of the mushroom to allow the spores to escape.

CAUTION: When these are in their spore stage, large clouds of spores can be released when the mushroom is touched. Don't inhale these spores, as there have been rare cases of where inhaling these spores can cause illness.

Stump puffballs often (but not always) grow in groups. They release spores from a tiny hole on their top.

EARTHBALLS

These odd mushrooms look a bit like potatoes scattered on the forest floor.

Habitat: Earthballs can grow from soil or from decaying wood and can grow alone, clustered, or near others.

Fruiting body: The shape of the fruiting body can be round, blob-like, or irregularly shaped, like a lumpy potato. The outside of the fruiting body can be scaled or smooth. It is usually yellowish to tan, brown, or dark brown on the outside. It will be quite firm, similar to a fresh potato. The inside is solid and starts out white, but very quickly will become purple or purply black as it ages. The purple-black layer will eventually become a powder (the spores). The fruiting body will eventually develop a hole in the top to allow the spores to escape.

Note: Avoid inhaling these spores, as they can cause an allergic reaction.

Earthballs sort of look like potatoes, at first glance. They are full of dark-colored spores when mature.

Corals and Clubs

Coral and club mushrooms really look like coral or something that grows from the ocean floor.

These mushrooms release their spores from their branches or club to reproduce. Coral and club mushrooms are usually fleshy or fragile, while some are firm. They can grow from wood or soil.

Golden spindles

Fairy fingers

FAIRY FINGERS

Fairy fingers are an accurate common name because this mushroom almost looks like thin fingers reaching through the soil!

Fairy fingers are saprobes *(say it, sap-robes)* and help break down or decompose leaf litter and other vegetation. They are often found growing in clusters. Sometimes, you can find several groups in one area!

Habitat: These will grow clustered or scattered in the soil under hardwoods or conifer trees.

Fruiting body: Fairy fingers are thin cylindrical or club-shaped mushrooms that can be up to 4 inches tall.

They grow upwards. The tips can be rounded or pointed. They are white or slightly translucent and turn yellowish at the tips as they age. These are also fragile and may break quite easily.

Spore color: Spore color is white.

Fairy fingers look magical when they emerge from the forest floor.

GOLDEN SPINDLES

The bright yellow or gold color of these mushrooms really pops when you spot them in the woods! There are several similar-looking mushrooms, so observe closely when identifying.

These mushrooms get their common name from resembling a "spindle," a spike-like stick used when making yarn.

Habitat: Golden spindles grow clustered and, on rare occasions, grow alone near others. They will grow from soil under conifer or hardwood trees.

Fruiting body: Golden spindles are very thin and cylindrical or flattened in shape. They grow upwards. The tips may be rounded or pointed and may become brown with age. These are also fragile and may break quite easily.

Spore color: The spore color is white.

Golden spindles are so brightly colored that they can be hard to miss!

VIOLET CORAL

Violet coral is one of the most eye-catching coral mushrooms due to its striking purple color on the forest floor.

This mushroom, like many other coral mushrooms, helps decompose organic matter, making it part of the forest "recycling crew."

Habitat: It grows alone or near others in soil or mossy areas.

Fruiting body: Violet coral is a vibrant purple in color. It grows upwards from one individual connection point but can branch off in different upward directions. It can grow up to 4 inches tall and 3 inches wide. The individual branches are very thin and fragile. The bright purple can fade to a dull purple as it ages.

Spore color: The spore color is white.

Violet coral really do resemble something out of a coral reef.

Other Mushrooms and Fungi

There are many mushrooms that don't fit into the common groupings of mushrooms. This section is for those special misfits! Because many of these mushrooms are so unique, their spore dispersal systems may be different from most mushrooms as well.

Morel

Lion's mane

MORELS

This is the mushroom that often gets people interested in wild mushrooms!

Habitat: Morels grow from soil near dead or living trees, conifer or hardwood.

Cap: The cap is not a typical mushroom cap. It has irregular honeycomb-like pits all over. The cap shape can be more cone-shaped or rounded. They can range in color from gray to tan to white, black, or brown. The cap is hollow. There is no real underside to morels, so they just flow from the cap, straight into the stipe.

Stipe: The stipe is whitish to a little yellowish and can be smooth or granular. It can also be hollow, all the way up into the cap.

Spore color: The spore color can range from whitish to yellowish or orangish.

Note: There is a half-free morel that has a longer stipe and shorter cap, where the stipe connects halfway up inside of the cap, giving that mushroom a bit of a fleshy overhang. Half-free morels are still morels, just with a slight difference in appearance.

Morel mushrooms (half-free morel shown on left) are really fun to see in the woods!

LOBSTER MUSHROOMS

This is one of the more unique mushrooms you can find! It is actually the result of two different fungi. This mushroom starts off as a white brittlegill or a white milky mushroom, then a parasitic fungus comes and attacks the mycelium of that mushroom and makes a lobster mushroom, which looks quite different than the host mushroom!

Habitat: These grow from soil near hardwoods or conifers.

Fruiting body: The fruiting body can be quite variable. Sometimes it resembles a typical mushroom shape with a cap and stipe, but other times it can be much more mangled in its shape or even ball-shaped on occasion. Whatever shape it takes will be bright orange, with possibly some white present and it will turn a reddish or magenta color as it ages. When fresh, it will be dense and firm, and as it ages it will become soft and squishy. If it is in a more typical mushroom shape, you may see some vein-like formations or bumps on the solid underside, but no gills.

Spore color: The spore color is white.

These are all examples of lobster mushrooms, which are produced when a parasitic fungus attacks another mushroom!

LION'S MANE

This wild-looking mushroom is actually a common favorite amongst mushroom hunters! Because of its very unique appearance, it has very few lookalikes! Similar-looking mushrooms have caps or are branched, similar to coral mushrooms. But incredibly, this is a toothed mushroom. It gets its common name for having a similar appearance to a lion's mane.

Habitat: Lion's mane grows from living oak or maple trees.

Fruiting body: This mushroom does not have typical features like a cap, underside, or stipe. Instead, the all-white fruiting body forms this roundish shape with dangling spines or teeth. This is considered a toothed mushroom. The fruiting body will turn brown as it ages and dries out.

Spore Color The spore color is white.

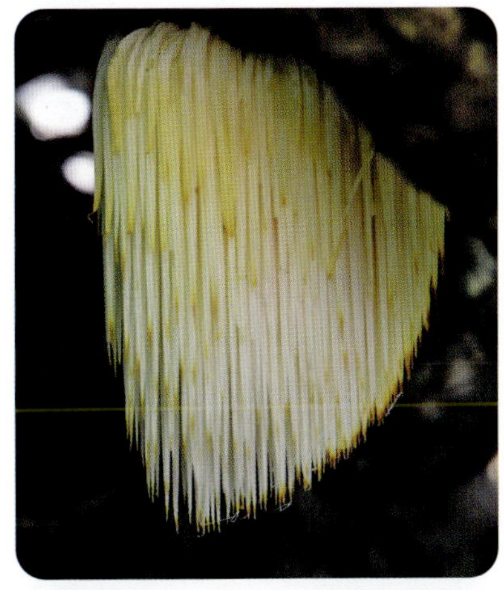

Lion's mane mushroom is so strange looking, it almost doesn't look real!

WOOD EAR

A mushroom that looks like an ear?! This jelly mushroom certainly does look like one! Jelly mushrooms are a surprising find, as they certainly aren't what most people expect when they think of a mushroom. Wood ears can also be really fun to play around with because they can be so jiggly!

Habitat: This mushroom grows from conifers or from hardwoods.

Fruiting body: Wood ear mushrooms are usually amber, tan, or a little whitish in color. One side of it (the side that usually looks the inside of your ear) will feel jelly-like or even gummy bear-like and will kind of fold and wrinkle. The other side will have pale, soft hairs that look like or feel like velvet with some veiny folds near where it connects to wood.

Spore color: The spore color is white.

Wood ear is well-named, and it is a fun, strange find.

OTHER MUSHROOMS AND FUNGI

ORANGE PEEL

These mushrooms get their common name because, from afar, they can easily fool people into thinking that they just found orange peels on the forest floor. Sometimes they even get completely dismissed because of this as well! Orange peel fungus is a type of cup mushroom and actually releases its spores from inside of the cup!

Habitat: Orange peel mushrooms grow in disturbed soil (on walkways, dirt roads, gardens), and they are usually found in overlapping clusters, but rarely are found individually.

Fruiting body: These mushrooms have a shallow cup shape and are usually small but can be up to a few inches across. They are bright orange and smooth on the inside of the cup and can fade to a yellowish color. The outside of the cup typically starts out white and fuzzy but will become smooth and orange with age. The margin of the cup can sometimes be a little wavy, not always forming a perfect cup shape.

Spore color: The spore color is white.

Orange peel fungus is brightly colored, but it is often small, so look closely!

EYELASH CUPS

Eyelash cups are small cup mushrooms that have small dark hairs on the outside and along the margin of the cup. These "hairs" really do resemble eyelashes! Because of these mushrooms' small size, you will have to look very closely to find them! You may even need a magnifying glass to actually see their "eyelashes" because they really are tiny sometimes!

Habitat: Eyelash cups grow clustered on wet or decaying wood.

Fruiting body: These shallow cup mushrooms are very small, only growing up to 2 centimeters across.

The inside of the cup can be bright red, bright orange, or orangish red. The outer surface is brownish or pale orange and is covered in small hairs that extend beyond the cup margin, giving that eyelash look.

Spore color: The spore color is white.

Eyelash cups are small, fascinating fungi. Bring a magnifying glass or a hand lens for a close look!

Slime Molds

Slime molds are not true fungi but are often lumped together because they are somewhat similar. Most slime molds grow in damp habitats, usually terrestrially (on the ground) or on wood. Slime molds have a fascinating life cycle. Some slime molds feed by forming large groups of cells called a plasmodium, which can move (very slowly). When mature, the plasmodium becomes net- or web-like, and then fruiting bodies (which carry spores) form on stalks. The spores help continue this life cycle. Other slime molds, known as cellular slime molds, feed by forming groups of amoeba-like cells (single-celled organisms). They can move too! Fruiting bodies on stalks develop from those groups of amoeba-like cells and produce spores

Note: The reproductive stages of slime molds (those that produce spores) are easier to spot, so we're only including photos of those here.

Chocolate tube slime mold

Dog vomit slime mold

WOLF'S MILK

These bubblegum-pink slime molds really stand out in nature! There have been recent studies around the world on this organism, and it has been found that there are many different species of wolf's milk slime mold. Scientists aren't even sure of exactly how many species there could be yet!

Habitat: Wolf's milk slime mold can grow scattered or clustered on decaying wood.

Fruiting body: This slime mold is actually pretty small but can occasionally grow up to half an inch across. They can range from pinkish gray to bubblegum pink to a reddish pink when young but turn yellow brown or olive brown as they age. When young, the squishy fruiting body holds a paint-like substance in the middle that can be various shades of pink. Eventually, that substance will become harder and turn into a purplish-to-grayish powder, which makes up the spores of this organism.

If you look closely, you might spot wolf's milk slime mold in the woods.

SLIME MOLDS

MOON POO

Moon poo has one of the silliest common names out there! Another common name for this organism is "the false puffball" due to its resemblance to puffball mushrooms, but "moon poo" is far more fun to say! This slime mold also has a unique relationship with a slime mold fly that will lay eggs in the spore mass. When the larvae hatch, they will feed on the organism. When the fly becomes an adult and emerges from the slime mold, it will carry the spores and help this slime mold spread to other places!

Habitat: Moon poo usually grows alone but occasionally grows near others on dead wood.

Fruiting body: This slime mold can look a little different throughout its life cycle. When young, it will be a rounded blob on the wood that is a creamy white color to a subtle pinkish color. Moon poo can have small or large lumps but tends to smooth out as it ages. It will be very moist, squishy, and easy to stick your finger into when it is young. It almost feels like pudding. The inside will be creamy white to a little pinkish. As it ages, the outside will turn silver, it will start to firm up, and the inside will start to darken to a brown color and eventually turn into a powder inside, which are the spores.

Also known as the false puffball, moon poo is a slime mold found on dead wood.

DOG VOMIT

This slime mold is named because it looks like vomit from a dog! Because of where it likes to grow, gardeners often stumble upon this organism and truly think an animal vomited in their garden, not realizing that this is actually a slime mold!

CAUTION: If you find this in its spore stage, please be cautious of breathing in spores, as it can rarely trigger asthma or allergies for some people.

Habitat: Dog vomit grows alone or near others on dead wood and occasionally plant stems or leaves. It often grows on mulch or wood chips.

Fruiting body: Dog vomit slime mold usually starts off bright yellow, sometimes a dull yellow, and usually appear as a lumpy mass that sometimes branches out on its substrate. It is moist, soft, and squishy when young. It has a unique soft-looking texture, and poking it feels similar to poking pudding. Your finger can easily go into the fruiting body when it is young. As it ages, it dries out and fades to a white, orangish, or pinkish color on the outside, and hardens. The inside eventually darkens to a black or dark gray color and turns to a powder, which is made of the spores.

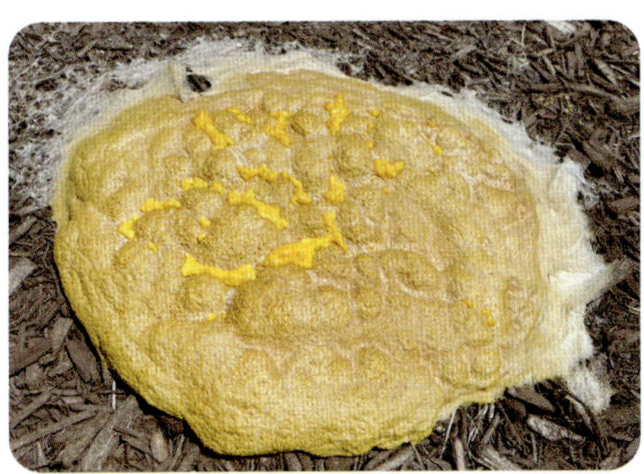

Dog vomit slime mold is also known as "scrambled egg" slime mold. It can look very different depending on what life stage it is in.

CHOCOLATE TUBE SLIME MOLD

This slime mold is named for being chocolate brown when mature, and it grows cylindrically.

Habitat: Chocolate tube slime mold grows in clusters on dead wood.

Fruiting body: Each individual "tube" is a thin, dark, thread-like structure near the base that turns into a thicker cylinder for the tips. The thin thread-like structure can be quite short compared to the longer, thick cylindrical tips. Each tube can be up to an inch long. When the cylindrical tubes are young, they can be whitish, yellowish, or pinkish, and they are soft and moist. When the tubes mature, they are brown, and although they are still soft to the touch, they are no longer moist. Chocolate tube slime molds are unique in that they hold their spores on the outside of each tube, so if you were to flick a mature cluster with your finger, you might see a puff of the brown spores or get the brown spores on your finger!

Chocolate tube slime molds are tiny, but really fun to find! And if you look closely on decaying wood, you may find them!

Projects and Activities

There are many fun activities that you can do with mushrooms! You can do some of these on your own or with friends or family! Many of these activities require the mushrooms to be picked, which is okay for the fungi because mushrooms are just the fruiting body. Only pick what you will use, though. Also, be aware of local rules and regulations about picking mushrooms, because collecting mushrooms is not allowed everywhere. (Collecting at parks might not be legal, for example.)

Shiny red hemlock varnish shelf mushroom

DO-IT-YOURSELF BIOBLITZ

A bioblitz is when a person or a group of people sets out to find, identify, and document as many things as possible in nature within a period of time. You can even do this in your backyard! Important: Disturbing mushrooms (say, by picking them) isn't allowed everywhere, so if you're not sure about whether you can collect in a given area, take photos instead.

Mushrooms picked for later photography.

THINGS YOU WILL NEED FOR YOUR OWN BIOBLITZ:

- A mushroom field guide or identification book for your region
- Paper or a notebook
- Pens, pencils, or markers
- A basket
- A camera or a smartphone

STEPS FOR YOUR BIOBLITZ!

Some mushrooms can be tough to spot, so observe carefully!

Choose your location! You can do this in your backyard or choose a nearby city or state park. If your city or state park has rules against collecting mushrooms, please skip any of the below steps that require collecting the mushrooms. If you choose a local park, having a map of the park may be helpful for navigation! It is also helpful to choose which portion of the area you might want to target beforehand.

Go to the location (with your parent/guardian) and start your search! Look high and low for mushrooms growing on trees (living or dead) or from soil. Some mushrooms can be small or like to hide in small crevices or under leaves, so take your time and look closely!

Take pictures! If you have a camera or a phone with a camera, take wider photos of the mushroom that include where it's growing from, then take close-up photos of all angles of the mushroom, being sure to include the cap, underside, stipe, and base.

Collect! Collect the mushroom and, while collecting, make note what the mushroom is growing from or near, as that can help identify them. Remember, mushrooms crush easily, so carry them in a basket or something similar to keep them safe. Try to keep them as intact as possible. If there are many of the same mushroom, only pick one of them. Dispose of all mushrooms outside when done.

Identify! Use your field guide to identify your finds! You can reference your notes or photos for information that may help you identify your mushrooms. If you can't identify everything, that's OK. Mushroom identification can be tricky, especially if the mushroom is relatively old.

Document! (optional) Have an adult help you upload your photos and information to iNaturalist (page 141) to participate in community science and document the mushrooms you found! If you choose not to document on an online platform, instead make a list of all the mushrooms you found and try to beat the number of species next time you conduct your own bioblitz!

SPORE PRINT ART

Spore prints are quite pretty, so why not use them for art?! We talked about how to make a spore print earlier (page 34), and making art from spore prints requires just a few additional steps!

USING SPORE PRINTS TO MAKE A PAINTING!

You will need:

- Blank canvases or construction paper. I recommend both black and white paper, and other fun colors.
- Paint
- Paintbrushes
- Cup of water to clean the paintbrushes
- Cup or bowl
- Mushrooms with gills or pores

STEPS FOR YOUR SPORE PRINT PAINTINGS!

Figure out what your spore print will represent in your picture. Spore prints make great flowers, suns, and

stars. Then, paint your images, leaving the spot for the spore print blank. I recommend doing several paintings at a time with different colored canvases to accommodate the different spore colors of the mushrooms you find.

While your paint is drying, you have a great opportunity to collect mushrooms. Try to find mushrooms the right size for your picture. It is helpful if you can identify your mushroom and know what color the spore print should be. If you know the spore print will be white, you will want to use a black or otherwise dark canvas so that the white spore print pops. If you use a white canvas and a mushroom with a white spore print, you won't get a visible print because the spore color will blend in with the white canvas. If this happens, you can reuse the canvas for another spore print.

If your mushrooms have a stipe, remove that.

Place your mushroom with the underside faced down where you would like it on your picture. Make sure your paint is dry before this step. If your paint is wet, it could dry to the mushroom or your cup or bowl in the next step.

Place a cup or a bowl upside down over the mushroom to block off any airflow. Let it sit overnight to give the mushroom time to drop spores. Do not disturb it at all during this time, or you may end up with a blurry or smudged spore print.

Reveal! Remove the cup or bowl to show your spore print. It's okay if it doesn't turn out perfectly because not all spore prints are successful. Just remember you can reuse the canvas if you don't get a visible print! Throw away the mushroom cap once finished.

USING SPORE PRINTS AND STENCILS TO MAKE A PICTURE!

You will need:

- Blank canvases or construction paper
- Stencils of your choice
- Mushrooms with gills or pores

STEPS FOR MAKING SPORE PRINT PICTURES WITH STENCILS:

Collect your mushrooms!

Select your stencils!

Select your color canvas or construction paper. If you can identify the mushroom and know what color spores it may have, that can help you choose the color of the canvas or paper. You don't want your spores to be the same color as the paper or canvas, or the spore print won't show up.

Place the stencil on the canvas or paper.

Select a mushroom that covers the stencil completely but doesn't go over the outer edge of the stencil. If the mushroom is too large for the stencil, the spores will go places you may not want them.

Remove the stipe of the mushroom if there is one.

Place the mushroom with the underside facing down over the stencil.

Carefully place a cup or bowl upside down over the mushroom to block any airflow.

Leave overnight and do not disturb! After that, simply remove the bowl and the mushroom, and then lift up the stencil to reveal your mushroom stencil art! Throw away the mushroom cap once you're done.

ULTRAVIOLET LIGHT AND MUSHROOMS

Some mushrooms (and other things in nature) react to ultraviolet light (aka UV) by almost glowing or reflecting a different color when exposed to this light. This is called biofluorescence. This can be caused by chemicals or compounds found in the mushrooms; sometimes, this UV reaction can even be used to identify mushrooms or lichen!

WHAT YOU WILL NEED TO FIND BIOFLUORESCENT MUSHROOMS:

- UV Safety goggles or glasses (available online)
- A UV flashlight (365nm recommended)
- A location to search (backyard or local park)

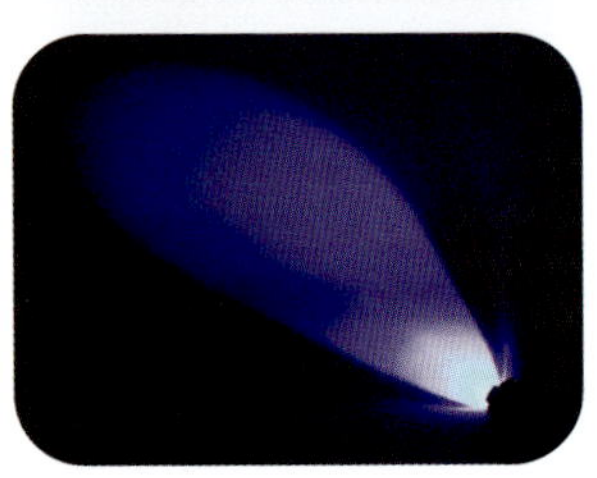

CAUTION: UV flashlights can be bad for your eyes. Please wear eye protection while using. Do not shine the light in your eyes, anyone else's eyes, or in the eyes of animals or insects.

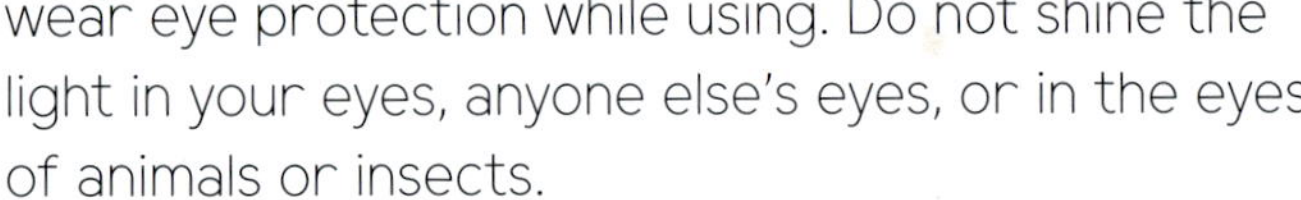

STEPS TO FIND BIOFLUORESCENT FUNGI:

Obtain your supplies.

Choose a location in nature to search.

Choose the time of day you want to search. If you go during the day, you can test each mushroom as you find them. If you go after dark, you can use UV light as your light source.

Put on your eye protection! Make sure anyone with you is also wearing eye protection.

Use your light! If you are searching during the day, you can point the light at each mushroom you find to see if you can see it reflecting or glowing a different color. If you are doing a search after dark, you can use the UV flashlight as a source of light and flash it towards the ground. You may see all sorts of mushrooms, lichen, or even plants that are biofluorescent!

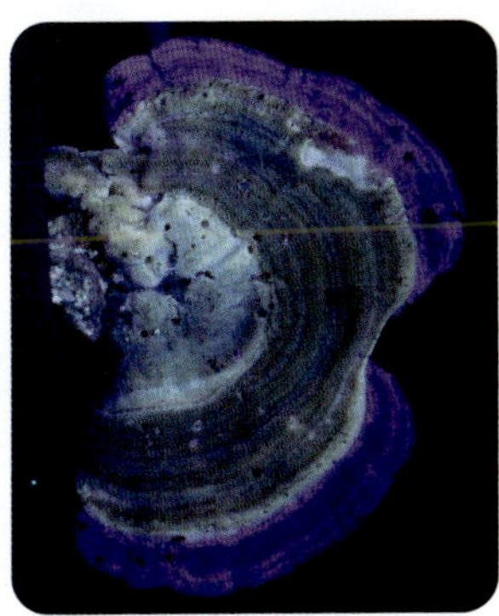

Take photos! (optional) Mushrooms that react to UV light make beautiful photos!

MUSHROOM RAINBOWS

Mushrooms of many different colors exist: When you're walking in the woods, you may see bright colors like reds, blues, greens, purples, yellows, and oranges. You can use those colors to make a mushroom rainbow!

TO MAKE YOUR MUSHROOM RAINBOWS YOU WILL NEED:

- Something to collect mushrooms in
- Mushrooms
- Camera (optional)

STEPS TO MAKE YOUR MUSHROOM RAINBOWS:

Choose where you will search for mushrooms! Please make sure you are allowed to collect mushrooms there ahead of time.

Go out and collect mushrooms of each color. You can collect many of each color or choose to collect one of each color.

Choose a nice location to lay out your mushrooms. Grassy areas are usually a good spot. You can also arrange them in order inside of your basket too or on a piece of paper or cardstock.

Arrange your mushrooms! You can arrange them according to the colors of the rainbow and in any shape you like, or you can get creative and choose a color pattern of your own!

Take a photo of your rainbow! (optional)

After you're done, discard your mushrooms back in the woods.

MAKING ART WITH ARTIST'S CONK MUSHROOMS

Artist's conk mushrooms are named because they are often used for art! Artist's conks are firm, shelf-like mushrooms that have a soft white pore surface on the underside. Those pores will hold any image you carve into them!

TO MAKE YOUR ARTIST CONK ART, YOU WILL NEED:

- Fresh artist's conks
- A firm, thin, rounded tool to etch your image (a ballpoint metal stylus works nicely, or even the top of the handle-end of a thin paintbrush would also work)
- A dehydrator
- A stencil (optional)

STEPS TO MAKE YOUR ARTIST CONK ART:

Collect fresh artist's conks (read about how to identify them and where they grow on page 70). Make sure the pores are bright white and a little soft to be sure they are fresh. Old specimens will not work. Also, be careful not to apply too much pressure to the pore surface, as it can bruise and possibly ruin your etching surface.

Use your etching tool to etch your art into the pore surface of the mushroom. If you aren't sure what to etch, you could even use a stencil as a guide. You don't need to apply a lot of pressure either. If you apply too much pressure, you may poke too deep into the mushroom.

After you are done etching your artwork, dry your artist conk in a dehydrator on low until completely dry. This may take 8–48 hours, depending on the size of your artist conk.

Display your art! Artist's conks look really good on a shelf!

Note: If you harvest artist's conks and can't etch them right away, you can store them in the fridge for up to 3 days and still use them.

MACRO PHOTOGRAPHY

Mushrooms make wonderful subjects for photography. Macro photography is when you take close-up photos of small subjects. This is usually done to capture unique features. Mushrooms have endless unique features that photograph well. You can even print out your macro photography to hang on your walls!

FOR MUSHROOM MACRO PHOTOGRAPHY, YOU WILL NEED:

- A camera or a phone with a camera
- Mushrooms

STEPS FOR MUSHROOM MACRO PHOTOGRAPHY:

Find a mushroom! Find what is unique about that mushroom.

Get up close! Go ahead and lie on your stomach to get a good look at all the features of the mushroom. Does it produce liquid? Does it bruise? Does it have a unique cap or stipe texture? Are the gills or pores pretty?

Find your angle! Choose what angle you want to take your photograph from. Also choose if you want the subject to be center or off-center. Move in or even use the zoom feature to get up close!

Take that photo! Make sure to hold your camera steady when taking your picture!

MAKING A MUSHROOM WREATH

Mushroom wreaths are such fun decorative items to make! They make great decorations to hang on your wall or to sit on a shelf!

TO MAKE A MUSHROOM WREATH, YOU WILL NEED:

- Mushrooms
- A dehydrator
- Plain grapevine or rattan wreaths
- A low-heat glue gun (use with an adult's help) or a strong quick-drying glue
- Other natural items like leaves, sticks, moss (from a craft store), and rocks are all optional

STEPS FOR MAKING A MUSHROOM WREATH:

Collect a bunch of mushrooms! Thin, small, shelf mushrooms are ideal, but any mushrooms can work!

Dehydrate the mushrooms in a dehydrator until completely dry. Timing may vary depending on how big the mushrooms are. This usually takes anywhere between 8 and 48 hours.

Come up with a plan! Choose where you want your mushrooms or other natural items to be placed on the blank wreath.

Start gluing each item in place. This is best done by applying the glue to the part of the mushroom that will be connected to the wreath, then hold the glue-covered spot on the mushroom to the part of the wreath where you want it to be. Hold the mushroom and wreath together until glue is dry for each item (this is why quick-dry glue is important). Apply extra glue where things feel loose or for larger items. Throw out any leftover or pieces that fall off.

Allow to dry fully overnight. Make sure everything is completely dry and sturdy.

Hang on your wall or display on a shelf. Make sure it's out of reach out of pets and/or children.

CAUTION: Please keep your decor out of reach of very young children or pets just in case a toxic mushroom was used in your artwork, and make sure all mushrooms are glued on securely. If you're concerned about safety, you can use fake mushrooms from a local craft store instead. They obviously won't need to be dehydrated.

Glossary

Ascomycete: Fungi with spores that develop in a sac-like structure, known as the asci

Basidiomycete: Fungi with spores that develop in club-like structures, known as basidia

Chitin: A fiber-like material that helps form the exoskeleton of arthropods (the group that includes spiders, insects, and others) and is present in the cell wall of fungi

Concentric: Circular or rounded zones

Conifer: A tree that has needles or scale-like leaves and forms cones; conifers are considered softwoods (as opposed to the hardwoods of deciduous trees).

Cylindrically: A shape that has straight parallel sides and a circular cross section

Cytoplasm: All of the material in a eukaryotic cell, enclosed by the membrane

Deciduous: Trees that lose their leaves, usually in fall

Decomposition: A stage of rotting or decay

Deliquesce: To become liquid during decomposition

Depress: To push or pull down

Eukaryote: An organism that has cells that contain a membrane-bound nucleus

Fungi: A taxonomic kingdom of eukaryotic organisms that includes yeasts, molds, smuts, and mushrooms

Hardwoods: Wood that comes from broadleaf, deciduous trees, such as oaks, maples, and so on

Guttation: The process through which plants or mushrooms release extra water, minerals, or chemicals

Macroorganisms: An organism that can be seen with the unaided eye (without a microscope)

Microorganisms: An organism that is so small that it can only be seen with a microscope

Mushroom: The "fruitbody" produced by some fungi (sort of like how an apple is the fruit of an apple tree); not all fungi produce mushrooms, but because they are easy to find and see, when people think of fungi, they usually think of mushrooms (as opposed to yeasts, molds, or other fungi).

Mycelium: The network of fine filaments that make up fungi; these are often known as mycelial networks.

Mycology: The study of fungi; scientists who study fungi are called mycologists.

Mycorrhizal: A fungus that grows in association with a plant that it has a mutually beneficial relationship with

Reproduce: When an organism produces more of its kind

Parasite: An organism that lives on or in another organism and takes nutrients from it

Polypore: Shelf-like fungi that grow from wood and often have pores on their underside

Saprobe: An organism that lives on organic matter (such as a dead log) and takes nutrients from it, contributing to decay and decomposition

Skirt: Part of a mushroom that covers and protects its underside; as the mushroom grows, this breaks, leaving behind a skirt- or ring-like material on the stipe.

Slime mold: A single-cell organism that is in the taxonomic kingdom Protista; slime molds are not fungi, but they have some fungi-like traits and feed on decaying matter, bacteria, or fungi.

Spore: Specialized structures that fungi and other organisms (such as slime molds) produce that enable it to reproduce

Spore color: Spores produced by fungi often have a specific color, and a spore print (see page 34) is one clue to help identify the fungi.

Stipe: The stipe or stalk of a mushroom

Substrate: The surface or material that a fungus grows from

Veil: A material that can cover up part, or all, of a mushroom

Yeast: An egg-shaped, single-celled organism that reproduces by budding or dividing and is capable of turning sugar into alcohol or carbon dioxide; people use yeast to make bread, beer, wine, and other foods.

Recommended Reading and Community Science

BOOKS

National Audubon Society. *National Audubon Society Mushrooms of North America*. Knopf. 2023

Kathy Yerich and Teresa Marrone. *Mushrooms of the Upper Midwest: A Simple Guide to Common Mushrooms*. Adventure Publications. 2020

Walt Sturgeon and Teresa Marrone. *Mushrooms of the Northeast: A Simple Guide to Common Mushrooms*. Adventure Publications. 2016

Alan E. Bessette, Arleen R. Bessette, and David P. Lewis. *Mushrooms of the Gulf Coast States: A Field Guide to Texas, Louisiana, Mississippi, Alabama, and Florida*. University of Texas Press. 2019

Vera Stucky Evenson and Denver Botanic Gardens. *Mushrooms of the Rocky Mountain Region*. Timber Press. 2015

David Arora. *All That the Rain Promises and More: A Hip Pocket Guide to Western Mushrooms*. Ten Speed Press. 1991

Noah Siegel and Christian Schwarz. *Mushrooms of Cascadia: A Comprehensive Guide to Fungi of the Pacific Northwest*. Backcountry Press. 2024

COMMUNITY SCIENCE

INATURALIST.ORG

iNaturalist is a community science website where users can upload photographs of plants, animals, and other living things, including fungi. This helps create a record of observations all over the world and helps science since there are far more regular observers than actual scientists. iNaturalist observations have helped spot introduced species, helped scientists expand range maps, and even spot new species! Better yet, iNaturalist is a great place to learn about your area and what's found there, and with your parents' permission, you can even upload your own finds. Who knows, you might find something really neat!

MUSHROOMOBSERVER.ORG

Mushroom Observer is a community science website dedicated to fungi! On the website, users can upload photos of their fungal finds and learn more about the fungi around them!

PHOTO CREDITS

Front cover photos: **Ariel Bonkoski:** top right (puffball mushroom), middle left (chanterelle), middle right (jelly leaf fungi); **Edwin Butter/Shutterstock.com:** bottom left (shaggy mane); **Tomasz Czadowski/Shutterstock.com:** bottom right (morel); **Mary Elise Photography/Shutterstock.com:** top left (chicken of the woods); **Amelia Design Art/Shutterstock.com:** background

Back cover photos: **Ariel Bonkoski:** top left (turkey tail); **Amelia Design Art/Shutterstock.com:** top background; **Gabor Magyar/Shutterstock.com:** middle right (deer mushroom decomposing a log)

All photos by Ariel Bonkoski unless otherwise noted.

Arleen Bessette: 29 (bottom); **Justin Hammers:** 46, 47 (bottom left), 55 (top, middle right, bottom right), 63 (all), 94, 95 (middle right), 101 (top); **Olga Katic:** 130; **Tavis Lynch:** 34 (bottom), 35 (top left, top middle, top right, middle), 40, 41 (top), 43 (top), 47 (middle), 49 (top), 51 (middle right), 54, 56, 62, 85 (bottom right), 99 (bottom right); **Brett Ortler:** 52; **Alan Rockefeller:** 24 (stinkhorn), 42, 43 (bottom), 48, 49 (bottom), 50, 51 (top, middle left), 60, 61 (bottom), 65 (middle, bottom), 68, 81 (middle right, bottom right), 87 (middle left, bottom), 90, 91 (top, middle left), 92, 93 (top, middle left), 95 (bottom right), 98, 99 (bottom left), 100, 102, 103 (top, middle left, bottom), 104, 105 (all), 107 (top, middle right, bottom right), 108, 109 (middle left, middle right), 112, 113 (middle left, middle right), 115 (middle left), 119 (middle), 129 (both)

Images used under license from Shutterstock:
Aleksander Bolbot: 32, 34 (top); **amedeoemaja:** 30 (middle); **Amelia Design Art:** 1 (background); **Andrea Danti:** 27; **ART-ur:** 14 (yeasts); **Artur Romanov:** 53; **Beach Creatives:** 88; **bob.leccinum.Robert Kozak:** 28 (top); **Bogdan Yakuba:** 121; **Cabin Boy:** 95 (middle left); **CampSmoke:** 143; **Camptoloma:** 14 (molds); **Designua:** 17; **DKeith:** 15 (lichens); **Donna Bollenbach:** 120 (top); **Elina Litovkina:** 11 (top); **emmerz:** 66; **flaviano fabrizi:** 71 (middle left); **Gabor Magyar:** 26; **godi photo:** 37 (bottom right); **GSDesign:** 6; **Helen Embry:** 37 (middle left); **Henri Koskinen:** 64, 71 (middle right), 77, 115 (bottom right); **Henrik Larsson:** 58; **HWall:** 114; **I.K.Media:** 31; **iwciagr:** 117 (bottom left); **JACGS:** 12; **JaneHYork:** 20 (stipe and skirts); **Jaroslav Machacek:** 57 (top); **Jennifer Wharton:** 97; **Jessi Jonas:** 89; **Joan Carles Juarez:** 41 (bottom left); **Jojo dexter:** 28 (bottom); **jopelka:** 82; **Josh Bukoski:** 95 (bottom left); **Julija Kumpinovica:** 65 (top); **Kandrah:** 47 (bottom right); **Kat Liepins Art:** 123; **Kathy D. Reasor:** 67; **Kulkova Daria:** 122; **Kyrylo Vasyliev:** 9; **LightHard:** 11 (bottom); **Lukas Jonaitis:** 110; **Marie Shark:** 39; **Martin Fowler:** 36 (top right); **Melica77:** 103 (middle right); **Morphart Creation:** 18; **N. F. Photography:** 91 (bottom); **NeilSaxon:** 37 (top left); **NK-55:** 71 (bottom right), 119 (bottom right); **nomis_h:** 93 (bottom right); **olko1975:** 8 (bottom); **Pumin Makaew:** 93 (middle right); **Reeves Photography:** 29 (middle); **ressormat:** 109 (bottom); **Ronapt1978:** 117 (middle left); **Sarapin Pavlo:** 83; **shoma81:** 10; **Spalnic:** 38; **Stefan Holm:** 44; **Thijs de Graaf:** 16; **Tintila Corina:** 41 (bottom right), 76, 109 (top), 119 (bottom left); **Tokariev Dmytro:** 128 (top); **Uhryn Larysa:** 57 (bottom right); **VectorMine:** 19; **Vitalii Hulai:** 96; **Vlad Kazhan:** 128 (bottom); **Volker Heide:** 111; **W van Dijk:** 91 (middle right); **Wirestock Creators:** 59

Turkey tail

About the Author

Photo by Brooks Bonkoski

Ariel Bonkoski is a self-taught mushroom identification expert who resides in Duluth, Minnesota. She has been studying fungi since 2016 and is now one of the most active mushroom identifiers in North America. Ariel has taught mushroom identification courses and led forays for colleges, public schools, mycological societies, and nature centers all over North America. Ariel is best known for her friendly and enthusiastic approach to teaching about mushrooms and fungi. She proudly participates in citizen science any chance she gets, in hopes to advance our knowledge about all things nature. She is an active Minnesota Master Naturalist, with a passion for learning, giving back to nature, and connecting people to nature. Ariel spends much of her free time camping, hiking, and foraging. She aspires to become an exceptional naturalist and promises to never stop learning. For more, visit Ariel's Mushroom Co: arielsmushroomco.com